BODY, SOUL & SPIRIT

MAKEUP OF MAN

DICK SORENSON

Compiled by
DONNA SORENSON & TAMI SORENSON GAUPP

Illustrated by
BECKY HANSEN

THE LANYAP LIFE BOOKS

Copyright © 2020 The Lanyap Life Books

All rights reserved. This book or any portion thereof may not be reproduced or used in any manner whatsoever without the express written permission of the publisher, except for the use of brief quotations in a book review.

Unless otherwise stated, all scripture quotations taken from the New American Standard Bible® (NASB), Copyright © 1960, 1962, 1963, 1968, 1971, 1972, 1973, 1975, 1977, 1995 by The Lockman Foundation. Used by permission. www.Lockman.org

PRINT ISBN: 9781736113912

eBook ISBN: 9781736113929

1116 Vista Avenue, #353, Boise, Idaho 83705

www.thelanyaplife.com

CONTENTS

How to interact with this material	5
1. The Composition of Man	9
2. When Sin Entered	17
3. Fellowship with The Godhead	27
4. Deceived But Redeemed	33
5. Satan Uses Sin To Manipulate	43
6. Empowered to Rule	65
7. Action Steps to Freedom	73
More Topics in This Series	79
About the Author	83
Special Thanks	87

HOW TO INTERACT WITH THIS MATERIAL

Our suggestion to you, as you read this material, is that instead of trying to search your memory and recall events or incidents in your life that the topics in *Journey to Wholeness* could apply to, pray this simple prayer:

> Lord, I thank you that my life belongs to you. All the restoration that you plan to do in my life is in Your hands. Holy Spirit, I give You permission to bring any and all events and situations to my mind that You want to heal and restore.

> *As Psalm 23:3 says, "He restores my soul; He guides me in the paths of righteousness for His name's sake."*

How to interact with this material

As He is leading, receive the restoration that happens as He helps you apply the principles in this series. Record the specifics of this restoration process. This will be your testimony of God's goodness and faithfulness to provide all of your needs. As He leads, you can share this testimony of God's miraculous provision with family and friends so God can use and bless it for generations.

Welcome fellow travelers on our journey to our inheritance as His sons and daughters!

Hiking toward hope on a personal journey to wholeness...

How to interact with this material

A message to you from Dick --

> This series is called *Journey to Wholeness* because it is the journey the Lord is taking me on to become whole. I find it has changed me and will do the same for others. I would say, as you discover these truths, take time with the Lord and ask Him to give you revelation on how to apply these in your own life. This is great preparation for ministering to others and training others to minister.
>
> May God guide and bless you as we journey together with Him. Welcome to The Journey!
>
> —*DICK SORENSON*

CHAPTER 1
THE COMPOSITION OF MAN

It is important to understand how we are composed and how we function.

> *Genesis 1:27 says, "God created man in His own image, in the image of God He created him; male and female He created them."*

We are created as a being, in God's image. God, the Creator, has created us after Himself and in His likeness.

> *Genesis 2:7 says, "Then the Lord God formed man of dust from the ground, and breathed into his nostrils the breath of life; and man became a living being."*

We see in this verse that man has three parts.

Man's body is formed from the dust of the ground. God breathed into man the breath of life. The word breath in Hebrew is the same as spirit. From God's Spirit, He imparts spirit into man's body. Man became a walking, living being, a soul.

Did you know there are three different Hebrew words used to describe the creation of man? One refers to the body, one refers to the spirit, and one refers to the soul.

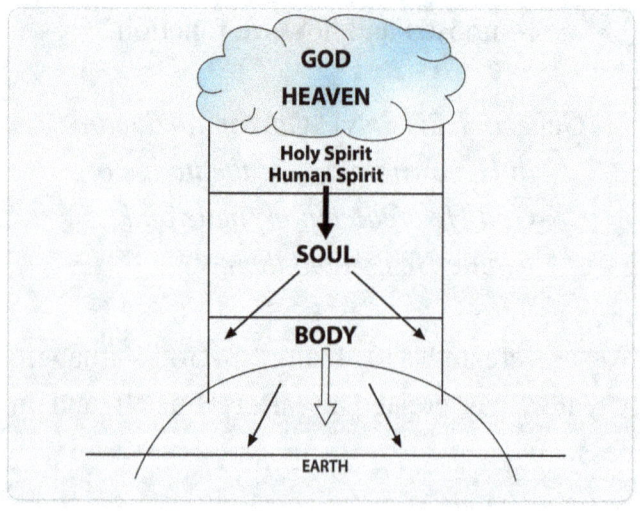

Image 1 -God Breathed His Spirit into Man

In this image we see God in heaven, as He

breathed into man the Holy Spirit (His Breath of Life), forming man's spirit. God made man's body from the earth and man became a living soul with a unique personality. There were no hindrances and no distortions, just open face-to-face fellowship between God and man. This was the relationship that God and man had in the Garden of Eden before sin was introduced by Satan.

Here is an image that gives another view.

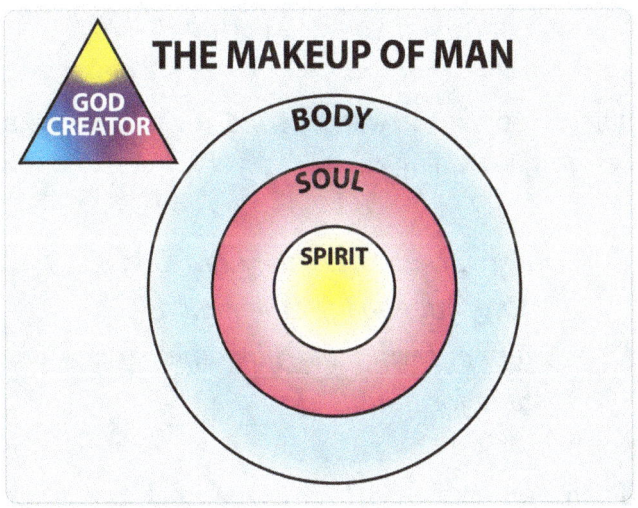

Image 2 -The Makeup of Man

When God initiated a relationship with man, He gave him authority (responsibilities) for the care of the Garden of Eden and all created beings. He also gave man freedom and He gave him the freedom to choose. God said they could eat from any tree of the garden except the tree of the knowledge of good and evil.

> *Genesis 2:16-17, "The Lord God commanded the man, saying, 'From any tree of the garden you may freely eat; but from the tree of the knowledge of good and evil you shall not eat, for on the day that you eat from it you will certainly die.'"*

Then God said it wasn't good for man to be alone so he created woman.

> *Genesis 2:18, "Then the Lord God said, 'It is not good for the man to be alone; I will make him a helper suitable for him.'"*

Then in chapter 3:1, we see that Satan as the serpent, approached Eve and asked the question, "Has God said you shall not eat from any tree in the garden?"

The woman responded and said, "We can eat from

any tree except this one, but if we touch it or eat from it we will die."

And so, the serpent said, "You won't die!" He inferred that God was being deceptive and wanted to keep them from becoming like God.

The result was that Eve and Adam made a choice to disobey and they experienced death. It affected their spirit, soul, and body, and also the earth. The open fellowship they had with God was broken. This included closure of man's spirit to open fellowship with the Holy Spirit. Man's soul had taken control and his spirit was almost nonfunctional. In fact, a basic meaning for death is to be separated and nonfunctional.

We are spirit, soul, and body.
But each part of us also has three parts.

Your body is composed of bones, flesh and blood. Isn't that correct? What about your soul? It also has three parts, mind, will and emotion. What about your spirit? It has three parts, intuition, conscience and communion. These are all part of your spirit.

Man is spirit, with a soul, dwelling in a body.

Let's go to Hebrews, just so we know it's not only in the Old Testament.

> *Hebrews 4:12, "For the Word of God is living and active and sharper than any two-edged sword and piercing as far as the division of soul and spirit of both joints and marrow and able to judge the thoughts and intentions of the heart,"*

According to Hebrews, there is a very fine line between the soul and the spirit. But there's a lot of interaction between the two.

> The heart of man is really a part of our soul and spirit. It is the understanding of our soul combined with the conscience of our spirit, with a connecting door of our will, forming the heart of who we really are. Therefore, this makes our choices eternally important.

Let's look at another verse.

> *I Thessalonians 5:23, "Now may the*

God of peace Himself, sanctify you completely and may your spirit and soul and body be preserved completely, without blame, at the coming of the Lord Jesus Christ."

God is interested in our body, He is interested in our soul and He is interested in our spirit.

When we are born again, we receive God's life and Spirit into our spirit. Our spirit becomes functional and alive to God. The redemption process begins in our spirit and our soul and our body.

God always starts with our spirit and begins the restoration of our soul. Finally, there will be a resurrection of our body. Sometimes we want to start with our body, but it doesn't work as well. As we go on, we find out there is always pressure from the outside that's trying to force us to conform to a certain way. But we will find there's a power from the inside to bring us into freedom.

Romans 12:1-2, "Therefore I urge you, brothers and sisters, by the mercies of God, to present your bodies as a living and holy sacrifice, acceptable to God, which is your spiritual service of worship. And do not be conformed to this world, but be transformed by the renewing of your mind, so that you may prove what the will of God is, that which is good and acceptable and perfect."

CHAPTER 2
WHEN SIN ENTERED

When God created Adam and Eve in the Garden of Eden, the Bible says, God had open and intimate fellowship with them. That means that on all levels of being, there was an open interaction between God and man.

Image 3 - Sin Brought Separation

In Genesis three, we see the account of unhindered interaction they experienced until sin entered in. When sin entered in, it distorted everything. But before that, there were no hindrances.

Just think of having no hindrance between you and God, always communicating, with no misunderstanding on your part. And in your emotions, you feel everything that God feels. You understand what God understands. You always purpose and will what God purposes. That's the way the fellowship was, but then there was a problem.

You know the story. Satan came as the serpent, he suggested that Adam and Eve eat the fruit of a tree that God had said not to. When they ate the fruit, sin immediately changed the fellowship they had with God. And that distorted everything.

> Our spirit immediately became clouded, our conscience became unclear, communion with God was broken and our intuition was faulty. We couldn't know what God wanted. Instead of feeling what God felt, we had our own feelings, mostly of fear, guilt, and pride. Then we started thinking, 'God's probably angry with me,' 'He may not like me,' and 'I'd better hide from Him.' Now our will isn't to do God's purpose: to come together in fellowship. Instead, we are thinking, 'I need to save

myself' and 'I need to hide behind something.'

The eyes of Adam and Eve were opened. They saw themselves as naked, and began asking, "What happened to our bodies?" They noticed they were changed.

In Hebrew, it says it differently. It actually says the covering of man was removed. I believe the covering was light. Jesus is the light. When the light comes and covers you, you are seen with God's brilliance. When Adam and Eve looked at each other they would see the light of God. When that was gone, they only saw each other, without God.

They said, "This isn't good. Something bad has happened." If they felt like that, they thought God would feel that way too. See how their thinking changed? It was different than God's thinking. Scripture says that at the same appointed time, God came to the garden. He said He was going to walk and talk with man in the cool of the evening. So, God came looking for man; but where was he?

God said, "Adam, where are you? Eve, where are you?"

And they said, "We're over here. We're hiding, behind the bushes."

"Why are you hiding?" God knew what was going on. But He wanted them to know they were hiding. God didn't hide, they did. God didn't withdraw fellowship, God didn't avoid them, even when sin came.

> **We need to understand that when sin has affected us, God is still pursuing us. He still knows where we are. He still calls out to us. He still seeks us.**

God said to Adam, "What happened to you?"
Adam said, "Well, I'm naked and I hid."

> **God always saw Adam as naked. Adams's looks didn't surprise God. You see, God knows exactly everything about us, everything. Nothing surprises Him. Sometimes we are surprised about ourself. And we say, "This is horrible. God probably can't stand this, so I'd better leave."**

God said to Adam, "Who told you, you were naked? Did you eat the fruit I told you not to?"
Adam, being the good responsible man said, "The woman You gave me, she did it!"

> **Do you know what the real accusation from Adam was? It was not about the woman, it was about God.**

Adam was, in essence, saying, "It wasn't my idea for You to give me this woman. You did it. And she messed up everything."

> **So, he was blaming God. Don't you think we do that periodically? We say, "God, I wouldn't be in this problem if it weren't for you."**

God didn't even argue with Adam, he just went to the woman. He said, "Women, what happened?"
She said, "The serpent did it."

Sin Entered the World

What we find is that each one of us blames someone or something else. That's what sin does, totally distorts truth and reality.

> *Roman 3:23 says, "For all have sinned and fallen short of the glory of God."*

There's not any person who has lived or ever will live, except for Jesus, who has not been affected by sin or acted out of sin.

> *Romans 5:12, "Therefore, just as through one man sin entered into the world, and death through sin, and so death spread to all men, because all sinned—"*

What we see is that sin entered into the world. When God created the world and created man, sin was not present. We also see that sin is not just an action. It wasn't just that man acted wrongly and did the wrong thing. The Bible says that through the wrong decision and action of that one man, the door was opened for sin to enter into the world and man's body. It's important to understand this.

Most of the time, Christians think that sin is just doing the wrong thing. They think that sin has to do with lying or stealing or some other bad action.

What we need to realize is that wrong actions are not sin. They are the result of sin.

The entire book of Romans is very good for showing us how sin operates.

Let's look at a few more verses.

> *Romans 5:18-19, "So then as through one transgression there resulted condemnation to all men, even so through one act of righteousness there resulted justification of life to all men. For as through the one man's disobedience the many were made sinners, even so through the obedience of the One the many will be made righteous."*
>
> *Romans 6:13, "and do not go on presenting the members of your body to sin as instruments of unrighteousness; but present yourselves to God as those alive from the dead, and your members as instruments of righteousness to God."*

> *Romans 6:16, "Do you not know that when you present yourselves to someone as slaves for obedience, you are slaves of the one whom you obey, either of sin resulting in death, or of obedience resulting in righteousness?"*

> *Romans 6:19, "I am speaking in human terms because of the weakness of your flesh. For just as you presented your members as slaves to impurity and to lawlessness, resulting in further lawlessness, so now present your members as slaves to righteousness, resulting in sanctification."*

> *Romans 6:23, "For the wages of sin is death, but the free gift of God is eternal life in Christ Jesus our Lord."*

Each one of these verses talks about how sin has come in and affected us. One greek word, translated as sin, is a word picture. It is a picture of a target or bull's eye.

You are standing with a bow and arrow. You are trying to hit the target, but you don't have the ability to pull the bow back far enough. You can't hold it steady enough. You're trying everything you can do, but you still miss the target.

Image 4 -Sin Prevents Us From Hitting the Target

Or it's a picture of a ten-year-old boy that is following his father and the father is walking across a river. There are stones in certain places. The father says, "Step where I step," as he is stepping on all the stones. The son tries to step on the stones but they are too far apart. Even when he jumps, he misses. He misses the mark. What this shows us is that even if we have the right desire we may not have the ability to do what is right.

CHAPTER 3
FELLOWSHIP WITH THE GODHEAD

Genesis three says the Face or presence of God came and He walked and talked with man in the garden. There was a triune fellowship between the Father, Son, Holy Spirit, and mankind. That fellowship affects our body, soul, and spirit. We are made for fellowship with the Godhead community.

There is an image on the next page, showing the triune fellowship of the Godhead. The Father, who represents the Face or presence. The Son represents the Voice, the talk, or the Word. The Holy Spirit represents the Way or the walk. Each one is able to interact with our being.

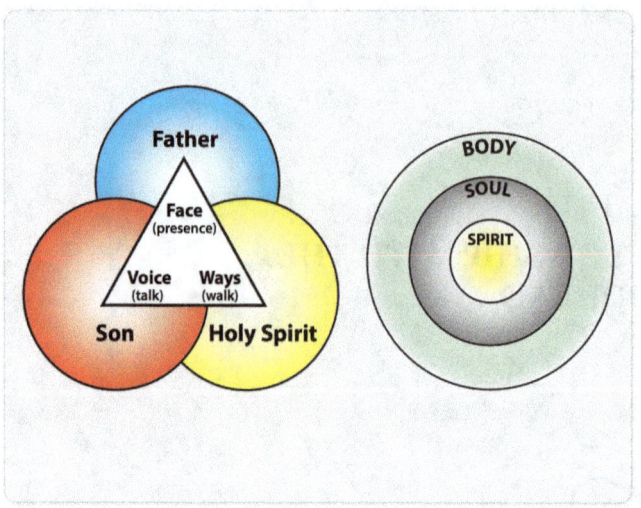

Image 5 - Triune Godhead and Man's Makeup

The Positive and Negative Spiritual Realms

As we discussed in chapter one, we are body, soul, and spirit. And there is a natural realm as well as a spiritual realm. There is positive and negative in both realms.

Just think about this in the physical world that we live in. There are positives and negatives. Is that true? Yes, it is.

In the spiritual realm that is also true. There is positive and negative. Satan and his dominions are the negative in the spiritual realm. We know who the positive is: it is God the Father, the Son, and the Holy Spirit.

Body, Soul & Spirit

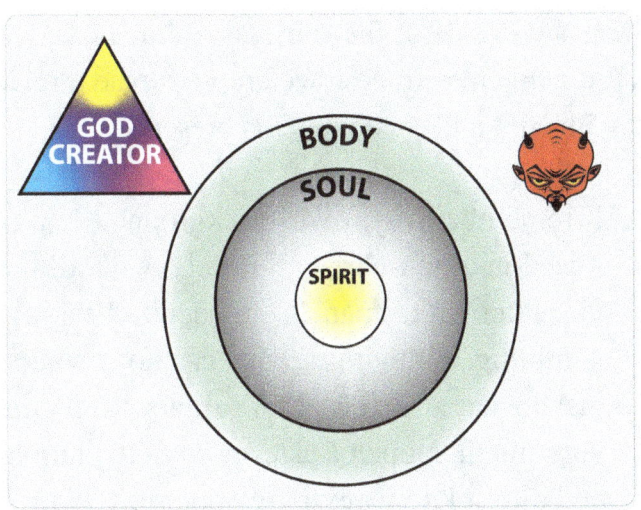

Image 6 - Positive & Negative of the Spirit Realm

Some might not understand this. They only believe in the natural realm, everything that can be measured by sight, touch, smell and sound. To them, there is nothing beyond the physical realm. Others think that everything in the spiritual realm is always positive. So, they pursue it. Some believe any spiritual activity connects them to positive energy, not knowing there is the dark side and negative energy.

There is always light and dark. God is light. In Him, there is no darkness. Satan operates in darkness, and his dominion is dark and negative, and results in destruction.

We may meet people who are contacting the spiritual realm, who say they are receiving direction, help, and enlightenment. But it doesn't necessarily mean it is the positive side of the spiritual realm. God gives us specific guidelines in how we are to pursue a relationship with Him and encounter His presence.

> I remember my own background. I was raised in a non-christian family, with all the vices known to man... the occult, drinking, gambling, brawling, and casino owners, just to name a few. My parents loved me very much. None of us ever went to church, and didn't know anything about it.
>
> My family was involved with the spiritual realm, psychic phenomenon, clairvoyance, and the like. So, even though I was not a Christian and didn't even know a Christian, I knew there was a spiritual realm because I was in contact with it. Everyone is searching for help and that's why Satan is called a deceiver. I was deceived. But, I learned eventually that there are two sides to the spiritual world. We need to be on the side of the positive, not the negative. God makes it very clear how He operates on the positive side.

Image 7 - God's Delegated Authority

God, who is the King and Ruler on this positive side of the spiritual world, created the earth and everything in it. He created man and woman together, and He gave them authority to rule over this earth. They were to represent God and light.

CHAPTER 4
DECEIVED BUT REDEEMED

*A*dam and Eve had the responsibility to represent God's nature and to bring His influence to all the earth. Everything that God created could fully blossom and reach its potential. He created it to be like it was in the Garden of Eden. Man, representing God, was supposed to bring total freedom and liberty to all of creation. But, what happened? Problems occurred!

When Satan deceived mankind, they actually gave up their authority, responsibility, and freedom. Their God-given authority to rule was forfeited to Satan because they believed his lies and accusations. Then, the world came under Satan's domain, and he became the default (illegal) ruler of the world. But God was and still is the King of all creation, including the earth.

Control is given to whomever you follow and obey.

Image 8 -Stolen Authority

Satan is called the prince of the power of the air and the ruler of this world. Here are a few scriptures that refer to this.

> John 12:31, " Now judgment is upon this world; now the ruler of this world will be cast out."

> John 14:30, " I will not speak much more with you, for the ruler of the world is coming, and he has nothing in Me"

> John 16:11, "and concerning judgment,

> because the ruler of this world has been judged."

> Ephesians 2:2, "in which you formerly walked according to the course of this world, according to the prince of the power of the air, of the spirit that is now working in the sons of disobedience."

So, we see that Adam and Eve gave Satan power over all the atmosphere of the earth. This did not eliminate God. God is still the creator. God has power and authority within Himself. God could have easily taken all this delegated authority back, but there would be a problem in doing that. He had already given it to man. Remember, man was created lower than the angels. So, man was weaker and yet God had given him authority to rule.

Satan was first known as Lucifer in the heavenly realm. He was created to lead all the angelic hosts in worshipping God. Instead, He made accusations against God, saying God was not the number one being. He saw that man was weaker and could not rule. He said, "You know I ought to be in control". Pride entered in as he compared himself with man and pride deceived and drove him to say, "I will become like the Most High, and I will ascend to the throne of the Most High." (Isaiah 14:12-14, Ezekiel 28:12-17)

So, if God by-passed man, Satan could say that God was going around what he already created. Satan was saying, "What you created does not work." But the Godhead already had a conference in eternity. They knew what they were going to do. Satan, as Lucifer, didn't know what was planned. He was very proud, thinking he was right and he had won. But, everything that was under his control became chaos, even the earth itself.

> *I John 3:8 says, "--The Son of God appeared for this purpose, to destroy the works of the devil."*

Jesus had to come and he had to come as a man. Jesus faced everything that Satan could throw at Him; all of Satan's temptations, accusations, power, and authority. Jesus took the power and authority away, as the Son of Man. Through Jesus' sacrifice, He redeemed what Adam, "the first son of man" had lost for mankind.

Image 9 -Authority Redeemed

It says in Galatians 4:4-7, that Jesus took the authority back because He earned it righteously.

> *Galatians 4:4-7, "But when the fullness of the time came, God sent forth His Son, born of a woman, born under the Law, so that He might redeem those who were under the Law, that we might receive the adoption as sons. Because you are sons, God has sent the Spirit of His Son into our hearts, crying out, "Abba! Father!" Therefore you are no*

> *longer a slave, but a son; and if a son, then an heir through God.*

Redeemed and Recommissioned to Rule

In Matt. 28:18-20, Jesus is talking to His disciples after the resurrection.

> *Matthew 28:18-20, "And Jesus came up and spoke to them, saying, 'All authority has been given to Me in heaven and on earth. Go therefore and make disciples of all the nations, baptizing them in the name of the Father and the Son and the Holy Spirit, teaching them to observe all that I commanded you; and lo, I am with you always, even to the end of the age.'"*

After He spent forty days with them, He was getting ready to bodily go back up to the presence of the Father. He said, "Now all authority has been given to Me, both in heaven and on earth, therefore I commission you to go out..." This is what we are to do. He re-commissioned us, who are born again, to represent our Father and bring liberty to all of His creation.

In I John 1:7-9 we see that we have full fellowship restored, with one another and with God.

> *1 John 1:7-9, "but if we walk in the Light as He Himself is in the Light, we have fellowship with one another, and the blood of Jesus His Son cleanses us from all sin. If we say that we have no sin, we are deceiving ourselves and the truth is not in us. If we confess our sins, He is faithful and righteous to forgive us our sins and to cleanse us from all unrighteousness."*

This is good news. Jesus redeemed our relationship and fully restored our fellowship with the Father. Because of that, you and I are recipients of God's mercy and grace.

As we receive His mercy and grace, we experience God's love, restoration, and recommissioning, as his sons and daughters. All of this happens because of the Father, Son, and Holy Spirit's eternal love and involvement together in pursuing us. You and I can experience this and learn how to live and walk in it. And we can share this Family Fellowship with one another.

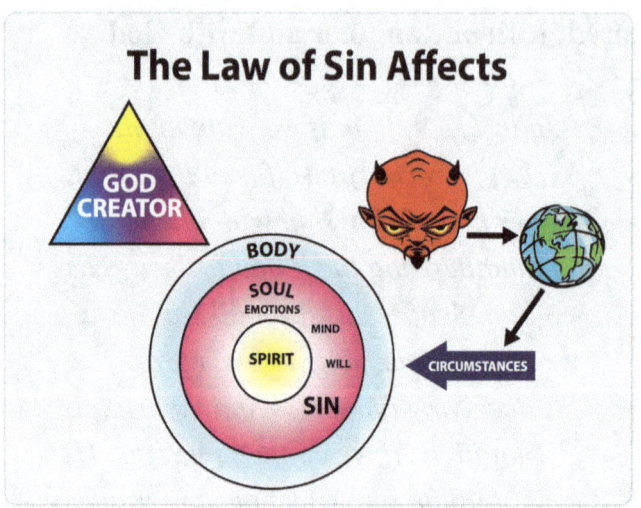

Image 10 -What the Law of Sin Affects

We're going to look at man as being redeemed.

When we are redeemed it means that we become functional in the physical and spiritual realms. Before you and I are born again, we're dead in our trespasses and sins.

> Ephesians 2:1, "And you were dead in
>   your trespasses and sins"
> Ephesians 2:4-5, "But God, being rich
>   in mercy, because of His great love
>   with which He loved us, even when
>   we were dead in our wrongdoings,

> *made us alive together with Christ*
> *(by grace you have been saved),"*

A better way to translate "dead" is to say we were nonfunctional. We talked about how sin distorted man, making our spirit out of tune. Do you understand that? It's like a television or radio program; if it's out of tune, you just get static. It has to be adjusted to get it back in tune.

Before we are born again, our spirit is out of tune with the positive side of the spiritual realm, but it's still functional to the negative side. It doesn't mean we don't exist when we're dead in our trespasses. It means we are not able to function the way God originally created us. Sin produces chaos and darkness. That means our soul is affected. As a matter of fact, the soul is the place where sin comes to reside.

CHAPTER 5
SATAN USES SIN TO MANIPULATE

Remember, sin is something that has come into the world. The scriptures that we referred to in Romans say that it came into each person. What that means is we're more open to the influence of the negative side of the spiritual realm than the positive. In the same way, you program a computer: when we are born into this world, we begin to experience the negative programming of this world. Sometimes this is called socialization. It's different for each one of us because of who we are. It depends on what culture you are in, what family you were born into, where you are in the family, your education, your environment, your experiences, and your perceptions.

Satan manipulates philosophies and belief systems in order to operate as the ruler of this world. He has that kind of influence through the negative side of the spiritual realm. We have grown up so immersed in it that we think it's normal. When we finally find out who God is and we encounter Him, our eyes are opened and we go through a transformation.

I was sixteen years old when I encountered God. Before that occurred, through the ruler of this world, I had already been programmed with a lot of sinful behavior. As a matter of fact, I learned how to respond to any situation. It was just like putting a program into a computer. Satan programmed me. All that was needed to get the program to play was to hit the right triggers.

Let me give you an example: I learned how to respond when someone resisted or attacked me. From the time I was a little boy, if someone took something of mine, I would not just let him have it. I would go get it back. And if he wouldn't give it to me, I would hit him and take it. If he was bigger than me, I would get a stick. I learned that what they did to me, I did to them. It's a good thing I'm redeemed now!

I had been learning to do this for sixteen years. It's a program that had been worked into me. The sin was operating and it had affected my mind, my emotions and my will. All Satan had to do was manipulate circumstances that caused a situation to affect my body and soul. This sent an impulse into my soul where the program was. That was the trigger. I didn't think about it, didn't even make a conscious decision with my will. It had nothing to do with my mind; it seemingly erupted out of nowhere. So that was the stimulus and the automatic response was immediate.

> Here is an example of how this works; I was standing in line to get some food. I was about twenty years old and this guy was behind me, pushing me. I kept running into people ahead of me. I kept telling him to stop. But, he did it one more time. It triggered the response. I turned around and I hit him, knocking him to the floor. Now, this guy was lying on the floor, with a split lip and his nose was covered with blood.
>
> I was looking down at this guy and Satan said, "You're not a Christian. Christians don't act like that."
>
> And I said, "Oh no, that must be right."

It took me a few years to find out what really happened. And why you and I have those kinds of responses within us. All of us have something programmed in us. Many times they are hidden. But Satan, who programmed us, knows where the triggers are. He manipulates circumstances and he picks the right place and time to do it; where it will cause the worst amount of damage to us and other people. But Jesus came to undo all of that.

Often, we believe that when you are born again, everything is solved once and for all. Well, that is potentially true. Because what Jesus accomplished on the cross and with the resurrection has set us free once and for all. When He finds us where we are, He says, "I'm going to set you free." Also, He says, "I'm going to transform you. I won't leave you the way you are." The first part is being born again. But His goal is to produce Christ in us, the Hope of Glory.

The Law of Sin

We find in Romans 5:12 and 19, that sin entered in through one man, Adam.

> *Romans 5:12, "Therefore, just as through one man sin entered into the world, and death through sin, and so death spread to all men, because all sinned..."*
> *Romans 5:19, "For as through the one man's disobedience the many were made sinners, even so through the obedience of the One the many will be made righteous.*

Body, Soul & Spirit

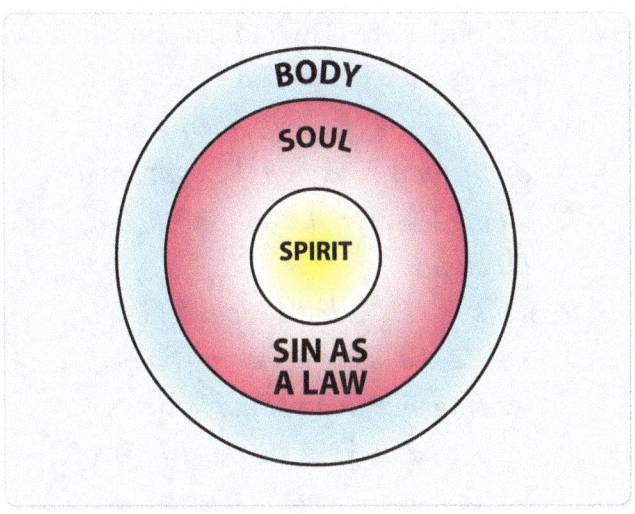

| Image 11 - The Law of Sin

Then we find out in Romans 6:12-13 that sin is like a slave driver. It will enslave you, causing you to produce evil and destruction.

> *Romans 6:12-13, "Therefore do not let sin reign in your mortal body so that you obey its lusts, and do not go on presenting the members of your body to sin as instruments of unrighteousness; but present yourselves to God as those alive from the dead, and your members as instruments of righteousness to God."*

Let's look at Romans 7:11 and 23. We find sin deceives and it kills. We also find that sin is a law.

> Romans 7:11, "...for sin, taking an opportunity through the commandment, deceived me and through it killed me."
>
> Romans 7:23, "...but I see a different law in the members of my body, waging war against the law of my mind and making me a prisoner of the law of sin which is in my members."

**In Romans 7:14-8:2
Paul is talking about himself.**

He says, "I don't understand my own actions. The very thing that I will to do, I can't do. The very thing that I decided not to do, I end up doing." Then in verse seventeen, he said, "It is no longer I that is doing the wrong, but sin that cohabits within me."

> Romans 7:19-20 "For the good that I want, I do not do, but I practice the very evil that I do not want. But if I am doing the very thing I do not want, I am no longer the one doing it, but sin which dwells in me."

We need to understand, Paul is beginning to make a distinction about his identity. Most of us just think about ourselves as a culmination of all that has happened in our lives. But Paul is indicating that after being born again, we become a new creation in Christ. And we are going to do new things. But there is a problem! Paul said, "I've got something dwelling in me that is in my soul that is trying to destroy me. It's not really me, but it's sin that dwells in me."

> *Romans 7:21-25, " I find then the principle that evil is present in me, the one who wants to do good. For I joyfully concur with the law of God in the inner man, but I see a different law in the members of my body, waging war against the law of my mind and making me a prisoner of the law of sin which is in my members. Wretched man that I am! Who will set me free from the body of this death? Thanks be to God through Jesus Christ our Lord! So then, on the one hand I myself with my mind am serving the law of God, but on the other, with my flesh the law of sin."*

Sin is an Entity

Sin is an entity of itself; just the way cancer can be a condition that lives within us.

We are not really the cancer; our body was not made to have cancer in it. But once cancer contacts and controls a certain area of our body, we lose control, especially under certain conditions. For instance, suppose a person goes to the doctor to get a physical examination.

He feels good. And he says, "Hi, doctor."

The doctor says, "Hi, let me examine you." After the examination, the doctor says, "You are sick."

You say, "No, I'm not. I feel good."

He says, "No, you're sick." And in order to prove it, he asked the man to do several things. Let's say the cancer has to do with his lungs. One of the things he asks him to do is take a deep breath, as deep as he can, ten times.

The man says, "Ok, fine, I'll do that." He finds he has a difficult time doing that, but he says he will do it anyway. The more he tries, the worse it gets.

Image 12 -Sin as an Entity Producing Destruction

That's the way you and I are with sin, when we come to God's word. The law is like the doctor saying, "Do these things" and we find we can't do them. As we try to perform right, we find we cannot do it. That just shows us that we have a problem.

> *Romans 7:19, Paul says, "For the good that I want, I do not do, but I practice the very evil that I do not want."*

Then in verse twenty-one of the same chapter, "I find then this principle to be true, that evil is present in me. The one who wills to do what's right or good. I see a different law in the members of my body and it wages war against the law of my mind and it makes me a prisoner of the law of sin."

> This is the first time anywhere in scripture that it is revealed that sin is a law and an entity. Here, the Holy Spirit began to give revelation. Sin is not just doing the wrong thing, it is not just an entity operating within us, it's not just a condition like cancer, but it is also a law.

This is an interesting thing to know, because you and I, most of the time, are trying to overcome the law of sin with the power of our soul. We try to overcome it with our mind, we try to overcome it with our will, or we try to overcome it with our emotions. We know that in each one of us, our makeup is a little different. Some people have more will power than others, some people have more emotional power, some people have more mind power than others, but all of them together are still only soul power.

What does the Law of Sin do?

Let me ask you this, do you know what the law of gravity is? We may not know all about the law of gravity, but we are aware that it works. We know that if somebody went up on a roof and jumped off, they would fall to the ground. They may say, "I don't believe in the law of gravity, I'm going to resist the law of gravity, I'm not going to let it control me," and they jump off and they flap their arms all the way down. Boom, they hit the ground because they are using their physical power to resist the law and it won't work.

Let me put it this way, I decide I'm going to overcome the law of gravity. I'm going to hold this Bible in my hand and extend it straight out from my side. I say, "See, I'm overcoming gravity, it can't control me. I am holding this book in the air." Gravity doesn't really care; it doesn't even pay attention or listen. It is always in operation. When I run out of power, things begin to go down; my arm has no more strength.

This is what the law of gravity says, "Anything composed of natural substance will be controlled and pulled down by gravity. Now, in order to overcome a law, you have to have another law. Something that has a different nature that is subject to that law.

For instance, there is a law of buoyancy. Hydrogen is subject to the law of buoyancy. It rises instead of falls. That means you can take a balloon that has the nature of something that is subject to the law of gravity, fill it with helium, let it go and it rises. If you take the same balloon and put your air in it, which is still subject to the law of gravity, it falls.

Image 13 -The Law of the Spirit vs. the Law of Sin

Our natural man and spirit, our own breath, even with the right motives are subject to the law of sin... like gravity. If you let go of that, what is filled with our natural spirit; the nature of man is always subject to the law of sin. And it will condemn you every time and fall to the ground.

But the new person we are in Christ, being a new creation, has a new nature and composition. It is subject to the law of the Spirit of life in Christ Jesus that sets us free from the law of sin and death. Just like helium in a balloon is subject to the law of buoyancy, it rises instead of being pulled down by the law of gravity. This means our air, that we blow into the balloon, is still subject to the law of gravity because of its nature and composition.

> *Romans 7:21-25, "When I come up against the Law I want to do good, but in practice I do evil. My conscious mind whole-heartedly endorses the Law, yet I observe an entirely different principle at work in my nature. This is in continual conflict with my conscious attitude, and makes me an unwilling prisoner to the law of sin and death. In my mind I am God's willing servant, but in my own nature I am bound fast, as I say, to the law of sin and death. It is an agonizing situation, and who on earth can set me free from the clutches of my sinful nature? I thank God there is a way out through Jesus Christ our Lord." (JB Phillips translation)*

We can make the right decision, we can set our will as strong as we want, we may align our emotions to feel the right way, and resist the law of sin as long as we can. But, when we run out of power, we will be subject to this law. And we prove this principle: You and I, in our human nature, are always subject to the law of sin.

> **Our body, soul, and spirit,
> without the Spirit of God within us,
> are always subject to the law of sin.**

Because you and I are born again, we are subject to a different law. It is the law of the Spirit of life in Christ Jesus. We have received a New Identity, a New Name and New Life from our Father. This nature is from heaven above and is always subject to a different law. It is never subject to the law of sin.

> *In Romans 8:1-2, Paul says, "There is now no condemnation for those in Christ Jesus. For the law of the spirit of life in Christ Jesus has set you free from the law of sin and death."*

The Sin Factory

> 66 The word *Sin*, singular, refers to the entity, the condition, and the law of sin. And the word *sins*, plural, is usually referring to the resultant reactions, behaviors, or products.

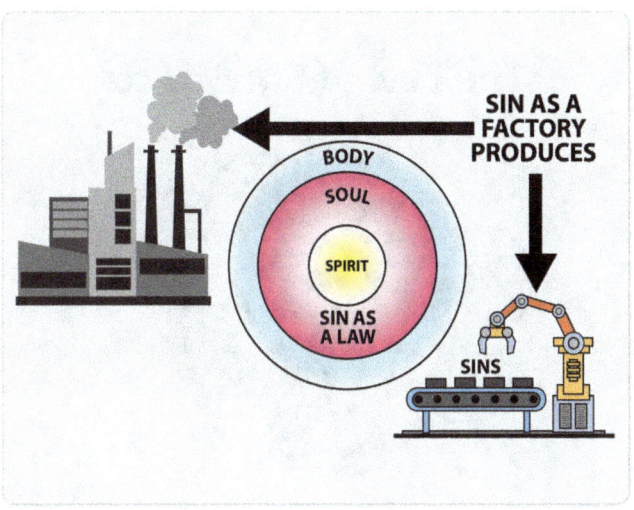

| Image 14 - Sin as a Factory

Sin refers to this entity and condition of this law. It's like a factory. Let's say that factory produces chairs. And you don't like chairs. You go everywhere you can and break chairs. Do you see what is happening? The factory is producing chairs, like *Sin*, produces *sins*. You try to stop all of the sins, but the factory of Sin keeps producing more.

**Wouldn't it be better
to shut down the Sin Factory?**

Image 15 -Sin Pollutes Man

This law of sin affects our spirit and darkens it. It affects our soul and it makes it so we are dependent upon ourselves. We use the knowledge of good and evil and our natural desires begin to control us. Our body is uncovered and vulnerable to the natural elements, weaknesses, sickness, disease, and decay.

This shows a change in man's being and in his relationship with God because sin had entered into creation. And it introduced an element of destruction and death. From this time on, all of creation was infected and ultimately experienced this chaos and separation until Jesus came to reverse these effects.

Sin As a Condition

Sin is also a condition, like a virus, that has all of these destructive, negative effects, not only in the body but also in our soul and spirit. As a result, we can be affected with seemingly unrelated symptoms.

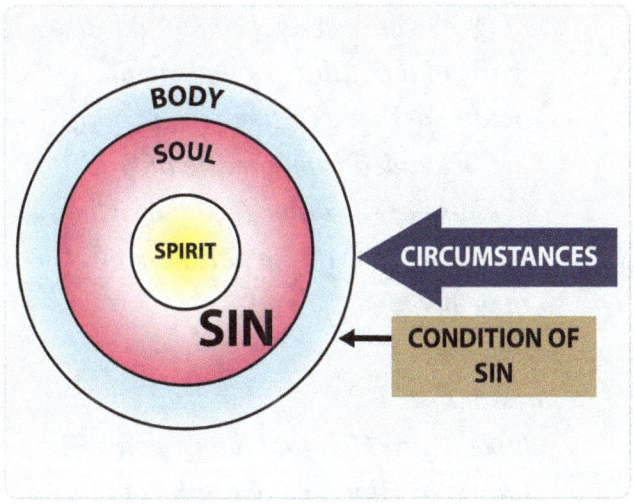

Image 16 -Condition of Sin

1. Affects the Mind

The mind can be darkened and have an incomplete understanding. It may also have distorted reasoning, clouded perception, and a lack of complete knowledge.

This can also cause a callousness of heart and a lack of compassion that affects our decisions and actions. So, the effects of sin and its resultant condition, are inevitable in this world without God's grace and Christ's redemption.

> *Ephesians 4:17-18, "So I say this, and affirm in the Lord, that you are to no longer walk just as the Gentiles also walk, in the futility of their minds, being darkened in their understanding, excluded from the life of God because of the ignorance that is in them, because of the hardness of their heart..."*

> *Ephesians 4:21-24, "...if indeed you have heard Him and have been taught in Him, just as truth is in Jesus, that, in reference to your former way of life, you are to rid yourselves of the old self, which is being corrupted in accordance with the lusts of deceit, and that you are to be renewed in the spirit of your minds, and to put on the new self, which in the likeness of God has been created in righteousness and holiness of the truth."*

Sin produces the desires of the flesh;
A combination of our emotions and our notions.

These desires of our flesh, push our will towards negative decisions and actions, the result is the works of the flesh or sin. Our physical bodies, in their weakened condition, are also susceptible to all of the effects of sin, which includes weakness and disease.

When we are led by the flesh, the results will always be negative and destructive. The only solution is to be led by the Holy Spirit as a new creation, which is Christ in us, the Hope of Glory.

> *Paul addresses this in Galatians 5:16,*
> *"But I say, walk by the Spirit, and*
> *you will not carry out the desire of*
> *the flesh."*

2. Affects the Earth

The Earth, as it was created by God, was perfect in every way, with no disease or decay. It was meant to be this way for eternity. But when mankind was deceived and sin entered in, it also entered into all creation.

Image 17 -Law of Sin Affects the Earth and the World

All of creation has been groaning, awaiting its salvation from the destruction it has been experiencing. As mankind's redemption continues, it will have a restorative effect on the earth itself. But one day God will recreate a new heaven and new earth that mankind will inhabit.

Sin Infiltrates the World

The word *world* is talking about all of the systems of society that mankind lives in and tries to control and develop on the earth. This includes environments, families, governments, culture, arts, business, and trade. Indeed, all systems that mankind lives in and relates to upon the earth. And sin is Satan's avenue to use power to flow through these systems and force diabolical destructive results. Deception, manipulation, control, and power are always involved in these systems.

But God sent Jesus to redeem people, the earth, and the world.

> *John 3:16 says, "For God so loved the world, that He gave His only Son, so that everyone who believes in Him will not perish, but have eternal life."*
>
> *Romans 8:20-29, "For the creation was subjected to futility, not willingly, but because of Him who subjected it, in hope that the creation itself also will be set free from its slavery to corruption into the freedom of the glory of the children of God. For we know that the whole creation groans and suffers the pains of childbirth together until now. And not only that, but also we ourselves, having the first fruits of the Spirit, even we ourselves groan within ourselves,*

waiting eagerly for our adoption as sons and daughters, the redemption of our body. For in hope we have been saved, but hope that is seen is not hope; for who hopes for what he already sees? But if we hope for what we do not see, through perseverance we wait eagerly for it."

CHAPTER 6
EMPOWERED TO RULE

Our human nature encompasses our body with its three parts, our soul with its three parts, and our spirit with its three parts. We are spiritual beings, with a soul (personality) and we dwell in a body. But these parts can get out of balance, especially, in the world systems that we live in.

When we get out of balance, negative long-term results may occur. But even when our body, soul, and spirit are functioning in harmony and good order, they are still subject to the law of sin because of their human nature and its composition.

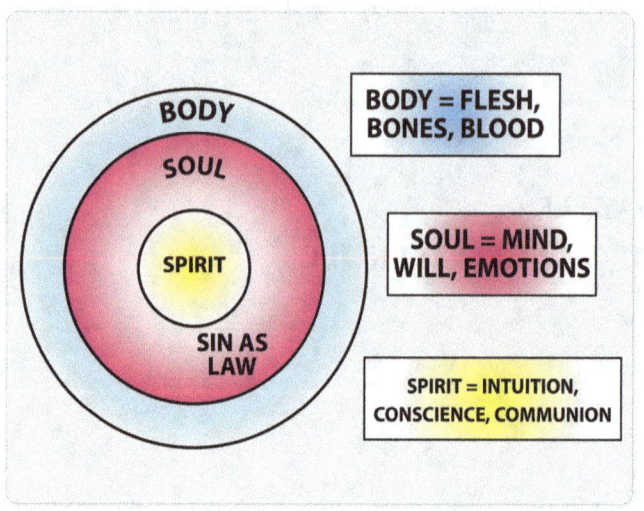

Image 18 - Our Human Nature

**The Life and Spirit of God is *uncreated* LIFE,
uncontaminated, uncorrupted,
and perfectly pure.**

Without the Spirit of God, our human nature, by itself, has no hope. When we become a new creation in Christ, we receive uncreated pure life from our Heavenly Father. That Life has always been and always will be. It is the Life of the Holy Spirit, Who begins to dwell in and through us. Then our journey from *captivity to conquest* as His sons and daughters has begun.

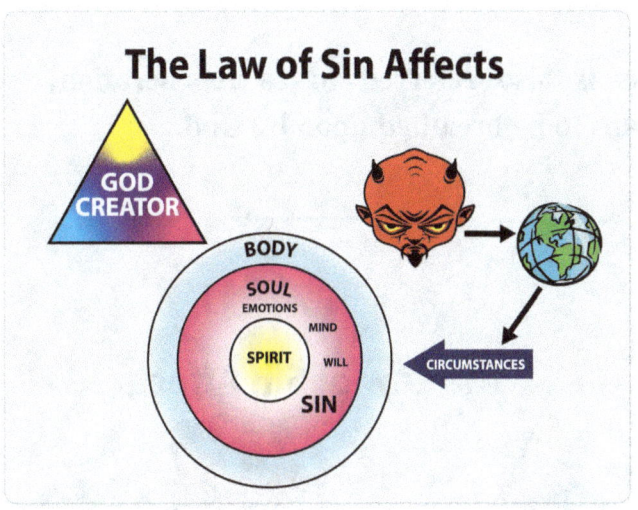

Image 19 -The Law of Sin Affects the World & Us

SALVATION

When we accept Jesus Christ as both Savior and Lord, we are born again. This term means that we receive God's seed of life from heaven. As a result, we become new creations and His sons and daughters.

We now are functional toward the positive side of the spiritual realm, which includes everything that has to do with our Father, His Son Jesus, the Holy Spirit, and the angelic beings. So, we become heirs to the throne of God, sons and daughters of the King of Kings and Lord of Lords. Now that we're tuned into His spiritual realm, we have access to the formidable power of the Holy Spirit to represent our Father.

This is also referred to as regeneration, which means to be breathed upon by God.

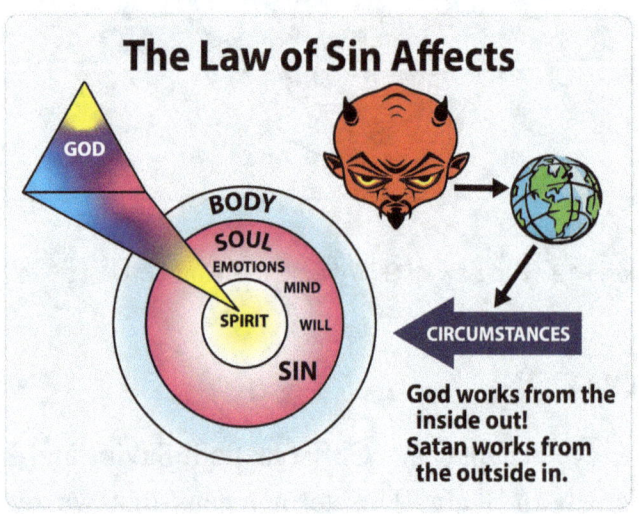

Image 20 -God Works from the Inside Out

In this diagram we see Satan having influence and control in the world. This allows him to manipulate destructive circumstances and trigger negative responses, even repeating them over and over, so we develop conditioned responses. These actions are produced by sin.

Under these conditions, Satan's control is secure

and destructive. But when we're saved, we receive a New Nature, the Holy Spirit, who comes to dwell in our renewed spirit from our Heavenly Father. Therefore, we can respond differently and not be controlled by preconditioned circumstances. So, we are on the road to transformation. We are growing in Christ because the Holy Spirit now lives in us.

> *Romans 6:12-14, "Therefore do not let sin reign in your mortal body so that you obey its lusts, and do not go on presenting the members of your body to sin* as *instruments of unrighteousness; but present yourselves to God as those alive from the dead, and your members as instruments of righteousness to God. For sin shall not be master over you, for you are not under law but under grace."*

We have a new law that we respond to. It's the Law of the Spirit of Life in Christ Jesus that sets us free from the Law of Sin and Death. This New Nature flows into us, through us, and out of us. It is a gift from God. It is the Way, the Truth, and the Life. JESUS!

> *Romans 8:2, "For the law of the Spirit of life in Christ Jesus has set you*

free from the law of sin and of death."

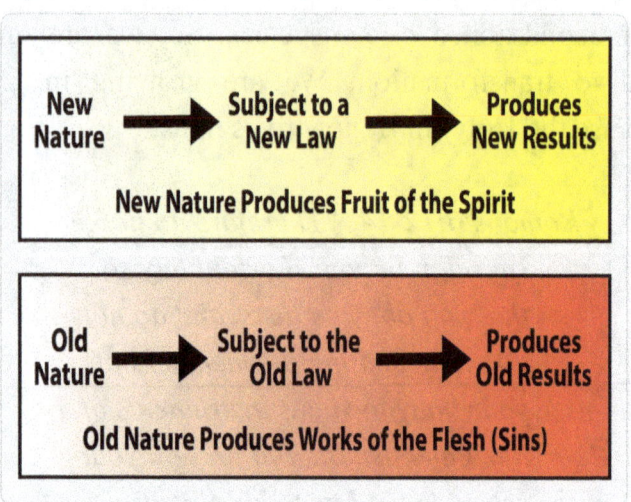

Image 21 -New Nature vs. Old Nature

Galatians 5:16-25, "But I say, walk by the Spirit, and you will not carry out the desire of the flesh. For the flesh sets its desire against the Spirit, and the Spirit against the flesh; for these are in opposition to one another, so that you may not do the things that you please. But if you are led by the Spirit, you are not under the Law.
Now the deeds of the flesh are evident,

which are: immorality, impurity, sensuality, idolatry, sorcery, enmities, strife, jealousy, outbursts of anger, disputes, dissensions, factions, envying, drunkenness, carousing, and things like these, of which I forewarn you, just as I have forewarned you, that those who practice such things will not inherit the kingdom of God. But the fruit of the Spirit is love, joy, peace, patience, kindness, goodness, faithfulness, gentleness, self-control; against such things there is no law. Now those who belong to Christ Jesus have crucified the flesh with its passions and desires. If we live by the Spirit, let us also walk by the Spirit. Let us not become boastful, challenging one another, envying one another."

CHAPTER 7
ACTION STEPS TO FREEDOM

We have discovered we have been formed in the image of God as a triune being. The entrance of sin has marred the originally designed function as God's children. But God had a plan to redeem us, transform us, and impart His life to us. This can never be contaminated or affected by sin. We can have His life grow in us. It will transform us into mature sons and daughters, expressing His life and love.

What are we to do?

We start the process by taking it to the Lord. Begin by using these questions to interact with Him and receive revelation.

Ask Him...

1. How is the law of sin affecting my life?
2. What programmed responses need to be revealed and replaced?
3. Is Satan accusing and prodding me to use the power of my soul (by focusing on specific sins) instead of receiving the life of the Holy Spirit and His power?
4. How can the law of Sin (the factory) be replaced by Christ's life in me? (refer to pages 59-60)

By choosing to yield your will to God and open your soul to receive the life of Christ from your spirit, you are using the Holy Spirit's power, instead of using your own soul power to try to control sins.

- Reckon your soul and the members of your body as dead to the Law of Sin and its effects.
- Reckon your soul and the members of your body as ALIVE in Christ and controlled by the Holy Spirit.

> Romans 8:2, "For the law of the Spirit of life in Christ Jesus has set you free from the law of sin and death."

Suggested Prayer:

> Holy Spirit, I open my spirit and my heart to receive more of Your power and life. With my will, I release You into my soul and my body, in order to be transformed into Your likeness.

Pray this prayer often.

PROCLAIM PAUL'S THREE DECLARATIONS

1. It is no longer I who live, but Christ who lives in me and the life that I now live in the flesh, I live by faith in the Son of God.

> *Galatians 2:20, "I have been crucified with Christ; and it is no longer I who live, but Christ lives in me; and the life which I now live in the flesh I live by faith in the Son of God, who loved me and gave Himself up for me."*

2. Christ in me is the Hope of Glory!

> *Colossians 1:27, "…to whom God willed to make known what is the riches of the glory of this mystery among the Gentiles, which is Christ in you, the hope of glory."*

3. **I am being transformed from one degree of glory to another by the power of the Holy Spirit.**

> *2 Corinthians 3:18, "And all of us, with unveiled faces, seeing the glory of the Lord as though reflected in a mirror, are being transformed into the same image from one degree of glory to another; for this comes from the Lord, the Spirit." New Revised Standard Version*

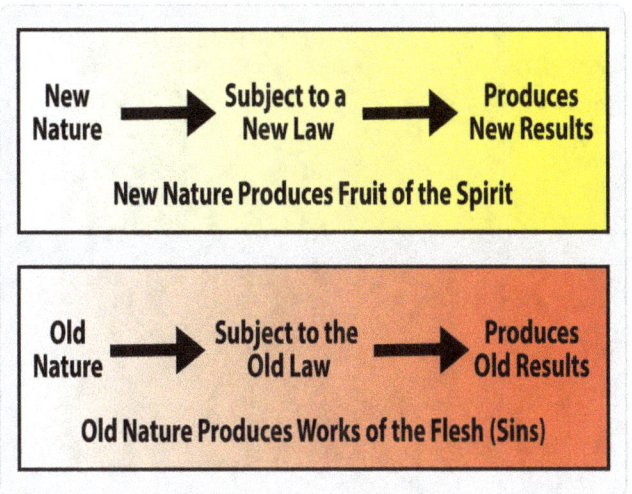

Image 21 -Old vs. New

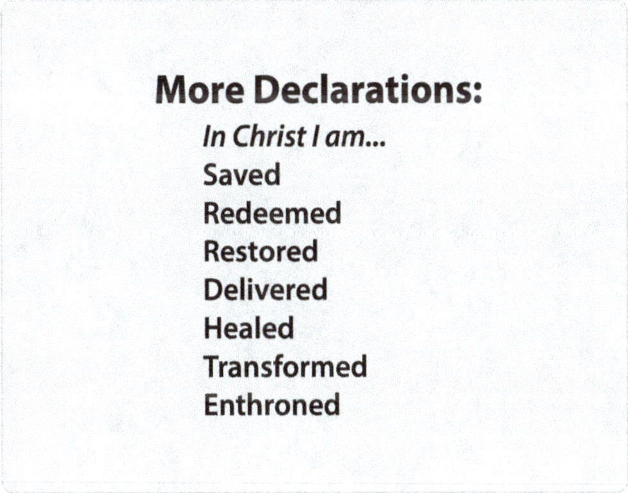

More Declarations:
In Christ I am...
Saved
Redeemed
Restored
Delivered
Healed
Transformed
Enthroned

Image 22 -Declarations

MORE TOPICS IN THIS SERIES

Thank you for your participation in this series.

If you've gained insight, we invite you to share your thoughts with us. You can do this in several ways:

- Leave a review
- Share on social media using the hashtags #j2wSeries, #dicksorenson, #thelanyaplifebooks and tagging us @thelanyaplife
- Contact us through our website thelanyaplife.com

Titles in this series: 13

The first six booklets in this series are centered on repairing, restoring, healing, and transforming areas of our past.

As we move on through the next 7 booklets, we'll be breaking free and rebuilding, replacing lies with truth, standing against the attacks of the enemy, pulling down strongholds, and we will be setting free what is bound.

That's good! It's not something we do just once; it's a lifestyle we learn to live with. Because of the rebellion, and the result of war Satan started in heaven, and brought to earth, you and I are in spiritual warfare. We will talk about spiritual warfare, look at the overview and then go over what is happening up close and personal in our lives.

Journey to Wholeness Series

1. Captivity to Conquest - *Preparing for the Journey*
2. Body, Soul & Spirit - *The Makeup of Man*
3. Transforming the Soul - *Memories & Interaction*
4. Forgiveness - *Surprising Benefits*
5. Accusations - *Believing a Lie*
6. Judgment - *The Boomerang Effect*
7. Brokenness - *Identifying Bruises and Wounds*
8. Healing of the Soul - *God's Intention*
9. Vows & Curses - *From Chains to Blessings*
10. Pulling Down Strongholds - *A Personal Privilege*
11. Binding the Strongman - *God Initiated Encounter*
12. Deliverance - *Steps to Freedom*
13. Areas of Spiritual Warfare - *Using the Right Tools*

About this Series

The *Journey to Wholeness* series is designed to be used as a guide or study to bring an individual into personal freedom and spiritual maturity. It is also designed to use as a study guide for a small gathering, home group, or a classroom setting. This material is a resource for leading a discipleship group, personal growth group or teaching a series for ministry training. Each topic is a separate booklet. Although all topics fit together to become the *Journey to Wholeness*, each can be discovered and applied separately to impart life, freedom and spiritual growth as needed.

This booklet is one of many topics in The *Journey to Wholeness* Course. The way this series became available is rather unique, since every single word in these booklets was spoken. The contents of this series has been compiled from PowerPoint slides, the seminar workbook and transcribed audio recordings on wholeness Dick delivered at a training center in Cairo, Egypt. This series is an original course of Dick Sorenson Ministries.

Hiking toward hope on a personal journey to wholeness…

ABOUT THE AUTHOR

Dick Sorenson was born in Twin Falls, Idaho, in 1946. When he was one day old, he was adopted into a loving non-Christian family and raised as an only child. At the age of three, his family moved to Nevada, where he grew up in the rough and tumble "wild west" environment for 10 years before moving back to Idaho.

Dick experienced a life changing encounter with Jesus Christ while reading the Gospels. He accepted Jesus as his Savior and was born again. A few weeks later, on Easter Sunday, he was baptized in water. It was also his 15th birthday. Two years later, he had another course-altering encounter that lead him to give up two college scholarships, one in nuclear physics and one in wrestling, to pursue full-time ministry. Then a scholarship was offered for him to attend Central Christian College of the Bible in Moberly, Missouri. He studied Hebrew for one year and studied Greek for three years. He furthered his education at Eastern New Mexico University, in Portales, New Mexico, receiving a double Master's Degree in Counseling and Theology. At age 20, Dick planted two new churches while still in college.

Since giving his life to full-time ministry since 1966, God has worked through him in resolving church conflicts, helping churches understand Biblical leadership, imparting vision, and as a resource for pastors and missionaries. In 1974, he started one of the first Christian Counseling practices in the State of Idaho, which served the community for 15 years. Traveling internationally since 1983, including ministry to unreached people groups, he has ministered in over 100 countries, training leaders and conducting seminars around the world. His non-denominational approach has reached across denominational lines, resulting in many lives touched through teaching, counseling, prayer and deliverance ministry.

Dick has a heart for the Nations and the workers in the field, taking teams for work projects, teaching the Word and prayer-walking in restricted access areas of the world. His passion is to prepare and urge people to step out in the call God has for them. He sits on three ministry boards and currently resides in Boise, Idaho, with his wife Donna, who he has been happily married to for over 55 years. They have two married children, two married grandsons and two great-granddaughters.

Dick and Donna live to fellowship—anywhere, anytime, and over coffee preferably!

SPECIAL THANKS

Many thanks to all those who have prayed, contributed to, and encouraged us to complete this series. We could not have accomplished this without your help. May God bless you on your journey... *What a blessing you all are to us!*

More about j2w can be found at:
www.thelanyaplife.com/j2w

www.ingramcontent.com/pod-product-compliance
Lightning Source LLC
Chambersburg PA
CBHW072207100526
44589CB00015B/2418